FERRARI F40

FERRARI F40

David Sparrow with
John Tipler

First published in Great Britain in 1994
by Osprey, an imprint of Reed Consumer
Books Limited, Michelin House,
81 Fulham Road, London SW3 6RB and
Auckland, Melbourne, Singapore and Toronto.

ISBN 1 85532 438 5

Editor Shaun Barrington
Page design Paul Kime/Ward Peacock
Partnership

Printed in Hong Kong
Produced by Mandarin Offset

The F40 driver needs to be quite circumspect about how hard he presses the accelerator. Because the F40 can easily get away from you, and on a wet road it can spin its wheels in the bottom four gears

For a catalogue of all books published by Osprey Automotive
please write to:

**The Marketing Department, Reed Consumer Books,
1st Floor, Michelin House, 81 Fulham Road, London SW3 6RB**

The Classic Italian Icon

Enzo Ferrari made his name as a works Alfa Romeo racing driver and later as its team manager during the 1920s. These were the halcyon days of the RLTF Super Sports and P2 racing cars. Later, they bore his emblem, the rampant horse, when he set up his own Scuderia Ferrari in December 1929.

The badge is now recognised by enthusiasts the world over. It was not a haphazard choice of logo, and there is some substance to the story of its inception. The black prancing horse symbol was bequeathed to Ferrari after a race win in 1923 by a Countess, the mother of World War 1 ace fighter pilot Francesco Baracca, killed in action in his SPAD S13; Enzo's brother had flown – and died – with him. The rampant horse, famed in art and sculpture from classical times, had been Baracca's squadron insignia – Squadriglia 91A – and was also used by the Italian airforce 4a Aerobrigata on F86A Sabres and F104G Starfighters in the late '40s and '50s. For his own racing team, Enzo Ferrari mounted the horse on a yellow shield, in deference to the town of Modena, with the initials SF for Sefac Ferrari beneath, and the shield was painted on either side of the car, just ahead of the cockpit.

He was born on 18 February 1898 at Modena, and the young Enzo's upbringing was perhaps more privileged than most, as his father ran a successful metal working business from the family home, and opened a garage in the early years of the 20th century. It was here that Enzo learned about automotive engineering, spurning the opportunity of studying it at college. After World War 1, he was turned down by Fiat, but took a job as the test driver of passenger cars derived from Lancia trucks. In Milan he met fellow tester Ugo Sivocci, and the pair teamed up in a CMN racer – Costruzioni Meccaniche Nazionali – for whom Sivocci worked, to tackle the Targa Florio. But for a local parade which delayed them, they would have finished seventh.

In 1920, Ferrari and Sivocci joined Alfa Romeo as works drivers, and Ferrari placed second in the Targa Florio. They were joined by Giuseppe Campari and Antonio Ascari for 1921, giving Alfa a particularly strong line-up. However, by 1923, Enzo's abilities as an administrator and co-ordinator took him out of the driving seat and into the role of team

The truth of the matter is that nobody builds supercars like the Italians, and Ferrari is the past master. The F40 in repose is a fabulous piece of composite sculpture

manager. That year, Alfa Romeo RLTFs swept the board in the Targa Florio, although Sivocci was later killed at Monza. The eight-cylinder P2, more of an out-and-out racer, took the World Championship for Alfa in 1924, and was raced with much success against Delages, Fiats, Sunbeams, Mercedes and Bugattis until 1929 when the six-cylinder 1750 was dominant.

At this point, Ferrari left Alfa – Nicola Romeo had just retired – but the parting was amicable and from then he simply ran the works racers. In 1932 came the twin-supercharged P3 Monoposto racers, and the car's designer, Vittorio Jano, was less amused that Ferrari was still running things. It was a short-lived racing car, because Alfa was taken over by the Mussolini-led Italian government in the wake of the Wall Street crash – which saw many manufacturers go down – and despite the enormous national prestige gained from success on the race track, the funds for developing the P3 ceased to be available. So Enzo Ferrari reverted to competing with the 8C 2600 Monza when Alfa withdrew the P3. He also went motor-cycle racing with a team of Rudges and Nortons. It was the beginning of the period of Silver Arrows domination, when Germany's Nazi-government sponsored Mercedes Benz and Auto Unions rose to dominate the Grand Prix scene. Ingenious and resourceful, Enzo Ferrari borrowed P3 components from Alfa Romeo and in 1935 built a pair of twin-engined 'Bimotores'. They could reach 200mph, and as such were the fastest cars of the day. But tyre development did not match such performance, and too many pit stops for tyre changes kept them out of the winners' circle.

In 1938, the factory decided to run its own competitions department, and although he was retained as team manager, Ferrari had to return all the works cars and equipment. There was some success nevertheless. The race organisers promoted a class of 'Voiturette' racing as curtain raisers to the Grands Prix, and Ferrari, together with Gioacchino Columbo, produced the Tipo 158. This 1.5-litre supercharged straight-eight, single-seater, was immediately a winner, and it was a certainly a crowd pleaser when the German cars were so dominant in the main event. (After the War, it would be unbeatable – until Ferrari's own creation gained sway.) However, before long, there was a clash of egos

The Ferrari F40 was the first genuine 200mph roadgoing supercar, and given an open stretch of uncrowded tarmac road, is the epitome of exhilarating motoring – a true driver's car. Nothing else comes close to matching the F40's ability to communicate with the driver, advising with an immediacy the road conditions and expressing through its steering and suspension how they may be dealt with; this is a typical Ferrari trait, and is derived from the race circuit. But it's even more manifest in the F40 because of its no-frills austerity

9

It isn't all a bed of roses with the F40. It's less at home on country lanes, where restricted visibility and tight corners require much circumspection. Potholes and ridges make the suspension and tyres thump and crash, and the steering wheel kicks back at the driver

Left

It's low, at 3ft 8in, 14ft 6in long, and 6ft 6in wide, and at 2425lb, its pretty light too. The predominantly wedge-shaped body has a fairly average drag coefficient of 0.34Cd. Its 2936cc twin-turbocharged, four-cam V8 motor develops 478bhp at 7000rpm. Imagine the racket at those exalted engine speeds – and as it's a Ferrari, you can safely take it up there; it's actually safe to 8000

Above

That means it has roughly 20 percent more power than the 288 GTO which preceded it, and more than enough to blur the scenery as you catapult dizzily towards the horizon

within Alfa Romeo over the intellectual Spanish design engineer Wilfredo Ricart, and Enzo quit, taking several leading, but more down-to-earth, engineers with him. The settlement with Alfa precluded him from building any cars in his own name for four years; however, nothing daunted, he put together a pair of sports-racers for the 1940 Mille Miglia from Fiat components and called them Vettura 815s.

Starting up in business

In 1946, the Second World War over, Ferrari set up in the Emilian provincial town of Maranello in the flat Po valley, some ten miles south of Modena, and close to the Appenine mountains. Enzo Ferrari had always been fiercely ambitious, independent, and passionate about powerful cars and forceful, talented driving. His first project was characterfully

Above
The chassis is composed of square-section tubular steel − a traditional solution − with composites bonded to it with structural adhesive

Left
The F40 is a combination of high-tech simplicity, in that its chassis construction and suspension set up are both traditional and finely-honed state of the art; yet they are unfettered by considerations of complex design

ambitious. The 125 Sport – originally conceived as a closed 'Berlinetta' coupe – was launched in competition in the hands of Franco Cortese at Piacenza on 11 May 1947. It was a curvaceous, long-bonneted open 'spider' or 'barchetta', with single aero screen, two headlights, and a large, almost rectangular radiator grille. It was powered by a 60-degree V-12 engine, of only 1500cc, which was cast in aluminium, and was a particularly sophisticated car. In 159 form – bigger 1900cc engine but same body – Raymond Sommer gave Ferrari his first international win at Turin on 12 October 1947. Ferrari's first shot at the big time was the Italian Grand Prix on 5 September 1948 with the 125 F1.

The first Ferrari coupe was the 166 Sport, its body built by Carrozzeria Allemano in Turin, and closely based on the original design

Right
There is a relatively simple ladder plan at the base, reinforced by a sturdy backbone and perimeter rails. A slightly smaller series of rails forms the windscreen surround, defines the door apertures, engine bay and front boot area. To this are added the composite sills, floorpan plates, spare wheel holder, and scuttle-bulkhead

Above
Thereafter the exterior panels are fitted – the ones you can see – which include the front and rear panels, doors, outer sills, rear three-quarter panels, rear valance, dashboard and roof. The F40 is the first non-racing car to feature these construction methods on a production line basis

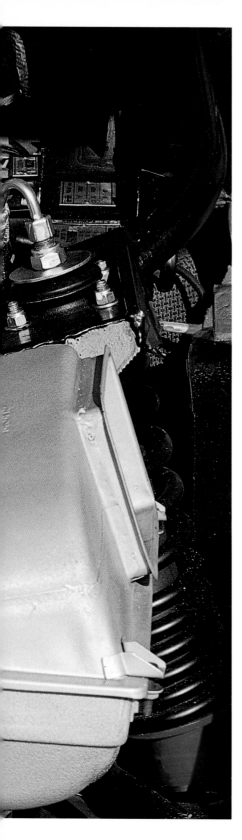

for the 125. Clemente Biondetti drove it to victory in the classic Italian road race, the Mille Miglia, on 2 May 1948. In 1949, a 166 MM roadster, driven by Luigi Chinetti and Lord Selsdon, won the first Le Mans 24 Hour race held after the war. But because of Jaguar's successes they would have to wait until 1954 for another win. In the 1951 event, Chinetti, who went on to found the North American Racing Team (NART), placed eighth. He also entered a 166MM coupe for Yvonne Simon and Betty Haig the same year which finished 15th.

Thus you can see that from the outset, Ferraris were about competition – and winning – and right up to the present day, there have

Above

The composite panels contribute to the F40's lightness and build strength. But Kevlar has a downside too, and is best used in small sections because of its inherent flexibility. Kevlar is extremely tough, but moves about because of the nature of its woven matting composition, so it doesn't stay flat for long, especially in broad flat planes where it forms ripples. If you push on a section of Kevlar, it yields, then springs back into shape, whereas a fibreglass panel is completely rigid

Left

The IHI turbos – that's Ishikawajima-Harima Heavy Industries – each delivers a boost of 16psi, each one feeding its own cylinder bank through a separate upwards-facing Behr intercooler. IHI, who began making turbos in Japan in 1939, also supply Fiat, Maserati and Lancia

been few concessions to anything other than sporting motoring of the highest standards. There have been a few relatively conservative body designs over the years, like the 166 Inter of 1948 with bodywork by Touring-Superleggera of Milan, Pininfarina's 400 Superamerica of 1959, and the 400 GT of 1976, also by Pininfarina; but these examples lack nothing in the way of elegance, and under the skin, they are all Ferrari. Because our subject, the F40 – and its predecessor the 288 GTO, and its progeny, the Evoluzione – are road cars, we will look at the development of these, keeping track of the sports-racers rather than the grand prix cars, although Ferrari history is inextricably linked with the highest levels of the sport.

Above
The light alloy V8 engine is probably the most exotic aspect of the F40: it betters the 288 GTO with a new crank, F1-derived fuel injection and ignition management system – the advantage of which is a higher 1.1-bar boost, so there's no need for a lag-inducing lower static compression ratio. There are also silver-cadmium con-rod bushes, hollow valves and nicasil liners

Right
These components all conspire to endow a comparatively lightweight car with a power-to-weight ratio of 450bhp per ton

The Carrozzerie

During his formative years as a manufacturer, Enzo entrusted body design to the leading Italian styling houses – 'carrozzerie', mostly based in Turin or Milan – including Stabilimenti Farina, training ground for many of the names who were subsequently to produce bodies for Ferraris. This is how specialist manufacturers got their cars built before mass production techniques became widespread: the factory built a traditional ladder chassis, fitted suspension and drive train, and the rolling chassis was dispatched from the Ferrari factory to receive its body and paint job at the *carrozzerie*. Stylists and bodybuilders employed by Ferrari included Farina proteges Alfredo Vignale, Giovanni Michelotti, (who sometimes

Above
Double wishbones constitute the suspension on all four corners, with concentric coil springs surrounding Koni dampers – with later models enjoying the sophistication of adjustable ride height dampers

Right
Top speed of the F40 is in excess of 200mph, which makes it on the books the fastest road car in production, although there are challengers for that crown like the Jaguar XJ220 and Lamborghini Diablo. Let's not mess about with 0-to-60mph times though; the F40 goes from 0-to-120mph in less than 12 seconds

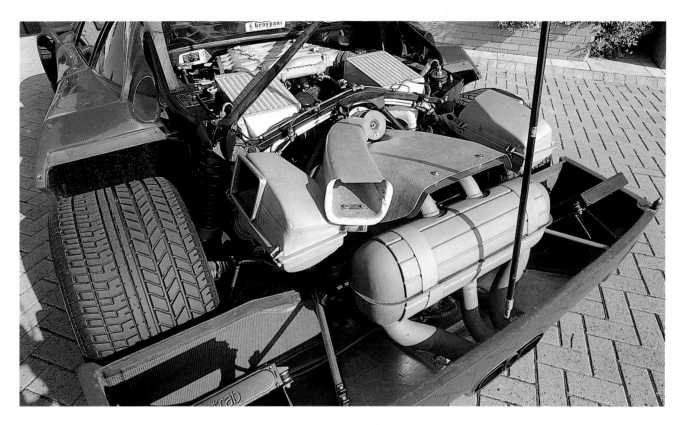

Above
The awesome stopping power is provided by four huge four-pot caliper Brembo disc brakes, which, as befits a race-bred car, are ventilated and cross drilled for lightness and heat dissipation

Left
Ferraris have long used the five-spoke star-shape road wheel. F40 steering is by unassisted rack-and-pinion

Right
Tyres are 335/35 ZR x 17s on 13 inch rims at the rear, with 245/40 ZR 17s on 8 inch rims at the front; they are Pirelli P-Zero, Goodyear Eagle GS-A, or Michelin MXX. Occasionally Bridgestone RE-71s are fitted

worked together, for instance on the 212 Inters), Mario Boano, who worked for Giacinto Ghia – (and whose interior designs favoured cloth to leather upholstery). And Ferrari also went to Touring-Superleggera of Milan, (who, with Vignale, built the early racing bodies). One Ferrari was bodied by Abbotts of Farnham, England, but from 1952, for a short while, most commissions went to Vignale, with the young Michelotti doing the styling. That year saw the first Ferrari styled by Giovanni Farina's younger brother Battista 'Pinin' Farina (later known as Pininfarina), and coincidentally, steering wheels moved to the left, having previously been located on the right of the car. The last Michelotti-Vignale creation, another 212, came out in 1953. Likewise, Touring's last road car for Ferrari was sold to Ford at this time. It was a 212 with a stretched 166MM Barchetta body. Production figures for these early years are instructive, for they reveal that Ferrari was much more prolific a builder of competition cars than road-going tourers. From 1949 to 1954, the firm built 250 sports racers, and some 200 touring machines.

There have been stylistic hallmarks from time to time, and the egg-crate grille first done by Pinin Farina on a 1952 212 Inter was the norm – and much copied – in the early '50s. The next phase in the Ferrari story was the 'America' series, so called because of the post-war fascination Europe had with Stateside attractions, not to mention the desirability of

marketing cars there. These fabulous cars set the trend in sports car design on both sides of the Atlantic: David Brown of Aston Martin bought a 340 America a year befor the 4.5-litre Lagonda V12 came out, and others including AC, Bristol and Chevrolet Corvette probably acknowledge a degree of influence from Ferrari. Ferrari's reputation blossomed at this time with the success of his Grand Prix cars, combined with other sporting successes like the MacAfee brothers' fifth place in the daunting 1952 Carrera Panamericana. Their mount was a 340 America with a rounded coupe body by Ghia; it was one of Ghia's last designs, although he did a few two-plus-two coupes as well.

Like Enzo, Pinin Farina's star was in the ascendant, and as well as doing more and more of the competiton cars, he styled most of the Ferrari America models produced during the '50s. Among these were cars like the '56 410 Superfast coupe, which clearly paid homage to the American preoccupation with fins. Its other striking feature was the pillarless 'Vutotal' wraparound windscreen. Others like the 375 America coupe of 1954 showed stylistic cues which would remain in place well into the '60s, although one which didn't was the curious 'grille-forward' snout of some of the 375 Americas. Possibly the most stunning of these '50s creations was the 375 Mille Miglia Berlinetta, shown at the Paris motor show in 1954. Its Pinin Farina body featured pop-up headlights,

Above

It wasn't long before F40 values were approaching £1 million. The bubble burst of course, and prices in 1994 are back to where the started – that is if you happen to see an F40 for sale

Above right

Access to the spartan interior is over a broad Kevlar sill, a distinctly awkward manoeuvre, but then you're getting into a virtual racer

Right

The dash is covered in grey cloth, which extends to the screen pillars and transmission tunnel. The roof has a sort of peppered plastic lining

trend-setting low-level radiator grille, aerodynamic tail fins done as sail panels, a sort of flying buttress arrangement echoed years later by Jaguar's XJS and the '68 Corvette. The whole ensemble lifted up as a tail gate. There were scallops with cooling louvres behind the front wheel arches too, a hallmark of the '56 Corvette.

Ferrari's America range was parallelled by its Europa range from '53 to '54, which used the same Lampredi V12, albeit scaled down to 3.0-litres. The newly reinforced chassis was the same, and there was little, if any, stylistic difference in the Pininfarina bodies. One obvious difference between Ferrari's cars was that the racers were invariably finished in bright red – the Italian racing colour – or at least an ostentatious colour, while the touring machines were, more often than not, painted a subdued and conservative silver, grey or dark blue.

In the mid-'50s came the 5.0-litre V12 Superamericas, again mostly bodied by Pininfarina, but with some dramatically finned cars by Mario Boano, plus the odd one under the auspices of Ghia. Competition

Above
By nature of its composite monocoque centre section, the F40's doors need a good slam to shut them, and are secured with quirky door locks, reminscent of early Minis!

Left
You have to raise the forward-hinged engine cover, rear wing and all, to check the engine oil in the dry-sump reservoir

Right

Lifting the engine cover is a hazardous operation, so big and light is the panel — it's easy for the wind to get underneath it

Above

The footwells and bulkhead are a mixture of composites and bare metal, while the padded Kevlar racing seats are savagely contoured to support the body at high speed. You can't adjust the seats for rake, but they move to and fro on their runners by a few knotches. Three indicator stalks sourced from the parts bins of Lancia and Fiat click the headlights onto dip and mainbeam, indicators and wash-wiper functions

models were generally built by coachbuilder Scaglietti at Modena, who also did some road-going commissions. The Superfast design was calmed down for '57. The Superamericas built between '59 and '64 were bold and brassy, providing more refinement, greater exclusivity, and greater performance – 340bhp – than the 250 GTs. The first of the series was the 400 coupe, which was notable for its huge, almost square radiator grille and twin headlights, comparable with a Facel Vega HK500, and certainly justifying the Superamerica nomenclature like no other Ferrari. It was powered by the 4.0-litre Columbo V12. Most of the subsequent cars were only different in detail to their contemporary 250 GTs, but Pininfarina dropped another stunner on the Turin Show in 1960.

Known as the Superfast II, it was the product of wind tunnel development, and looked like a mobile rugger ball, so dramatic were its curves. Capacity was lifted to 4.6-litres, and the concept underwent three revisions; Superfast II and III had retractable headlights, while the more conventional Coupe Special Aerodinamica – for limited series production – came with either fared-in headlights or exposed, with

Above
Until you're familiar with the switchgear, it's possible to retract the pop-up headlights by mistake when going on or off main beam

Right
Neither steering column nor driving seat is adjustable, so the driver has to compromise

appropriate grille treatment. Superfast VI, built on the chassis of the abandoned Superfast II, featured quadruple headlights. Superfast III had a grille opening which was thermostatically controlled. In 1962, the chassis was lengthened, but there was still not enough space for rear seats. There were 31 Coupe Special Aerodinamicas in this Superamerica range, and just three Superfast prototypes.

The charisma of the engines

Another significant aspect of Ferraris, and notably Enzo's competition cars, is that virtually without exception, they have used Ferrari engines rather than off-the-shelf motors like the ubiquitous Ford-Cosworth DFV of the '70s.

Above
Rearward vision from the driving seat is less than adequate, with the door mirrors pointing down the engine air intakes, and the driving mirror compromised by the louvres of the rear screen-engine cover and stabiliser bar, as well as showing too much of the rear wing

Left
Central binnacle houses the main instruments; tachometer is red-lined at 7750rpm, speedo to 225mph/360km/h, plus boost gauge for turbos and water temperature

There have been three different V12s, two flat-12s, two V8s – including the Vittorio Jano-designed unit of the Lancia D50 which Ferrari inherited when Lancia was broke – four V6s and two straight-fours. Enzo had a reputation for hiring and firing according to the successes achieved, and Columbo was ousted when his 1500cc V12 engine failed to win any of the early post-war grands prix. Ironically it was Columbo's pre-war design for the Alfa Romeo 158 engine which was the one to beat. Ferrari's next engine man was the analytical and practical Aurelio Lampredi, who reasoned that a freshly designed, large capacity unit could beat the supercharged cars. The 4.5-litre V12 was the answer, and it beat the Alfas in 1951. Lampredi's 2.0-litre four-cylinder F2 engine ruled the roost in '52 and '53, with Ascari, Farina, Taruffi and Hawthorn winning 30

Above
Pedals are drilled for lightness. This preoccupation with reducing unsprung weight extends to the omission of door handles – wire pulls have to suffice – an absence of internal adjusters for the rear-view mirrors on the doors; there is no carpet or interior light, so you can forget all about electric window lifters and a radio

Left
You don't buy this kind of car for hedonistic effects such as these. A legacy of its Italian origin – and Mediterranean climate – is a rudimentary air conditioning system, dispensing either hot or cold air and controlled by two small rotating knobs above the three vents

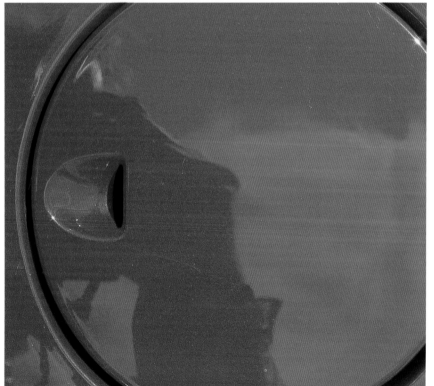

Above

With no hesitation, the F40 starts up on the coldest mornings, and it's unfazed by stop-start traffic snarl-ups, which would have had a Daytona oiling its plugs, and is smooth and tractable at low speeds

Left

Twin fuel fillers – tricky to unlock – replenish the F40's 26.4 gallon petrol tank; such is its potential frugality that a range of 600 miles is quite possible

Right

Turn the ignition key and you hear the fuel pump whirring from somewhere behind you. Just below the key and to the left is the rubber starter button; press it and the engine roars instantly

out of 33 World Championship qualifiers in two years. When Lancia's racing organisation was drawn into the Ferrari fold, the ageing Jano came too, and Lampredi went to Fiat.

The very nomenclature of Ferrari models is based on the cubic capacity of either the whole engine, or, confusingly, of just one cylinder. Thus you have the 365 GT4 BB, for example, which stands for 365cc per cylinder – it's rounded up to the nearest whole number, and you have to know it's a flat 12 to get the total cubic capacity – Gran Turismo four-cam Berlinetta Boxer. The Dinos have a simpler system; the 246 Dino has a 2.4-litre V6 engine, and this identification system carries on through the 308 GT4 series. The 512 BB is a 5.0-litre flat-12, but the F40 is the oddball in representing 'Ferrari – 40 years'. Strictly speaking, it

Above

The absence of sound-deadening on the Kevlar body panels makes road noise from the outrageously wide – 335/35 at the rear – Pirelli P-Zero tyres almost deafening. At low revs, the engine's V8 wail is almost drowned

Left

Maximum torque of 425lb/ft is reached at 4000rpm, and maximum power is 478bhp. No wonder the F40 is so fast – it weighs less than 22cwt, scarcely more than a ton. Above 3000rpm, acceleration is furious, and demands total concentration from the driver lest the car get the upper hand. With race-bred wishbone suspension all round, the ride is uncompromisingly hard and unrefined

should be called a 308 – that is, a 3.0-litre V8.

Ferrari's philosophy was to pass on the fruits of racing success to his touring cars, and the majority of road-going Ferraris of the first half of the 1950s used derivatives of Lampredi's 4500cc 1951 Grand Prix V12 engine. The 250 GTs used the short V12, originally designed by Ing. Columbo as a sports racing engine, but now slightly de-tuned. There have really been five categories of Ferrari: the single-seater racing cars for F1 and F2; the sports-racers for contesting the World Championship for Makes – Le Mans-type cars; grand tourers for doing just that; roadsters or spiders for fast fresh air motoring; and there is another category of sports cars, derived more overtly from competition. The F40 is one of these animals.

Like other car design geniuses such as Chapman, Ferrari was never content with the looks or performance of his cars, soon becoming bored or looking for improvements. Thus most cars, especially the prototypes, were the subject of constant change and refinement, much of it carried out on the basis of trial and error. If something went awry in a race, it was the driver who was blamed first. And if he couldn't be faulted, the engineer responsible got a roasting.

Sporting pedigree

Probably the most significant car, in terms of establishing Ferrari as a builder of serious grand tourers which could be race competitive from the word go, was the 250 GT. The Pinin Farina bodywork was very similar to the 250MM and 375 MM coupes of a couple of years before. Launched in 1954, the Marquis de Portago gave the 250 GT its first victory at the Nassau speedweek in 1955. But it would not come into its own until the Le Mans race in 1959, when 250 GTs outshone the Testa Rossas and came in third and fourth overall.

Until very recently, the 24 Hours was the benchmark for excellence in sports car racing, but during the '50s it was as yet the province of Jaguar D-Types, Aston Martins, and some equally wonderful Ferraris and Maseratis. These included the latter's fabulous V8-engined 450S, and the equally gorgeous, low-slung Ferrari sports racers of 1957, the Tipo 500 TRC (Testa Rossa), 290 MM, 315 S and 335 S. The 1958 Le Mans 24 Hours was won by Olivier Gendebien and Phil Hill in a 250 TR, with Gendebien and Paul Frere winning the event in 1960 in another Testa Rossa. It was a vintage year for Ferrari, with Maranello occupying six of

Steering the F40 demands a certain amount of give-and-take. Hold the wheel lightly and feel the road wheels jump and wriggle over every undulation

Above
The prancing horse makes a quantum leap over the F40's aerodynamics

Above right
Betraying its racing heritage – as if any reminder were necessary

Opposite above
F40 logo stamped its mark in special celebration of Ferrari's 40 years as a manufacturer of supercars

Right
Slatted rear window over engine bay dissipates some of the heat – but doesn't help rear vision

the first seven places. (Jim Clark/Roy Salvadori's Aston Martin was third).
Privately entered Ferrari 250 GTs were fourth, fifth, sixth and seventh.
The same pairing (Gendebien/Frere) took the honours in the 1961 race
in one of the aggressive looking shark-nosed 250 TRI/61s.
Mairesse/Parkes were second in a similar car, with the Noblet/Guichet
250 GT third overall and class winner. To underline the potential of the
250 GT, the Rob Walker car of Stirling Moss/Graham Hill had out-run
the second-placed TRI/61 until its retirement. Also promising before its
retirement was the works 250 GT, driven by Tavano/Baghetti, which was
the prototype for the forthcoming 250 GTO. It had special Pininfarina
bodywork and a Testa Rossa engine.

In what must be seen as the halcyon days for Ferrari, Gendebien/Phil
Hill clocked up another victory at Le Mans in 1962, this time in a 4.0-litre
330 LM sports prototype – the last for a front-engined Ferrari. Not far
behind was the class-winning 250 GTO of Jean Guichet/Pierre Noblet,
with the Ecurie National Belge GTO third. The true harbingers of the
F40, the mid-engined 246 SP prototypes were too undeveloped to last
the distance, and another Ferrari legend, the 250 GT 'Breadvan' also
failed to finish. These were also great times for Ferrari in F1, with
Champion Phil Hill, Taffy von Trips (to lose his life at Monza) and Richie
Ginther dominant in the 'Sharknose' 1.5-litre V6-engined 156; the engine

Above
*Tail light and indicator sourced from
family parts bin*

Above right
*The F40 is a mass of interesting
geometric shapes – like the air intakes
on the flanks*

Right
*The prancing horse on a yellow shield
have been Enzo Ferrari's symbol since
1929*

was based on the Columbo design, Carlo Chiti was the master tactician behind the operation.

Ferrari's seventh Le Mans success came in 1963, with the Italian duo Lorenzo Bandini and Ludovico Scarfiotti sharing SEFAC-Ferrari's 250 P. Not only was it the first mid-engined win at the Sarthe circuit, but a mixture of GTOs, 250P and 330 Ps filled the first six places. It was probably Ferrari's greatest triumph. Maranello topped the podium for the fourth successive occasion in 1964 with the works 275P of Jean Guichet/Nino Vaccarella leading home another two mid-engined prototype 330Ps. The fourth-place 250GTO of 'Beurlys'/Lucien Bianchi was beaten by Dan Gurney's Daytona Cobra. In 1965 the fantastic Ford-Ferrari duels were in full swing. The battling Titans pitted GT-40 against 275, 330 and 365 P2s, but it was the less radical 250 LM of Jochen Rindt/Masten Gregory which took the honours, followed home by Ecurie Francorchamps' similar car. The Mairesse/'Beurlys' 275 GTB came an unexpected third – a front-engined car was doing well to be so highly placed by now, and the Belgians fought off five Daytona Cobras into the bargain. The first Dino also appeared at Le Mans in '65.

Ford was victorious in 1966 with the Mark II GT 40s taking the first three places, as almost all Ferraris retired. The elegant front-engined 275 GTB of F3 stars Piers Courage/Roy Pike saved Ferrari honour by taking

the GT class and eighth place overall. In '67 Ford's triumph was repeated by the Mark IV Ford, but the fabulous P4 Ferrari – surely the raunchiest looking sports racer ever – of Mike Parkes/Ludovico Scarfiotti took second place at an average of 134mph. The Belgian P4 of Mairesse/ 'Beurlys' was third overall. The next phase of works involvement on the international circuit was from 1970 to '71 with the 512 S; these cars placed fourth and fifth at Le Mans, but were fundamentally outclassed by the 4.5-litre Porsche 917s. 1971 saw the first appearance of the 375GTB 4 Daytona, driven by Bob Grossman and 'Coco' Chinetti Jnr. It won the Index of Thermal Efficiency. With a change in the prototype capacity limit from 5.0- to 3.0-litres, Ferrari had virtually a clean sweeep in 1972. It won everything except Le Mans, which it opted out of, having already clinched the title and not wishing to risk its reputation by running the fast but fragile flat-12 312 P/B over 24 hours. However, the Daytona of Andruet and Ballot-Lena finished fifth at Le Mans and won the GT category, heralding a new era of success in the Touring division. The victory went to Matra, which was then enjoying a spell at the top. They were followed by another French team, Alpine-Renault, in '78, when Ferrari's opposition came in the form of the Daytona's mid-engined successors, the 365 GT 4B and 512 BB. With successive Le Mans victories going to Porsche and Rondeau, (the latter's success being the

first time the event had been won by a constructor driving his own car), Ferrari had a lean time of it.

Private entries in the early '80s consisted of 512 BBs with various degrees of body modifications, skirts and wings, but none were outstanding performers. The running gear may have been different, but these were undoubtedly the ancestors of the F40 in terms of their visual aggressiveness.

Classic cars

Meanwhile, to return to '50s road car development, variations on the coupe theme by Mario Boano won the GT category in events as disparate as the Nürburgring 500kms, Tour de France and the Alpine Rally; a Boano 250 GT won the Acropolis Rally outright in 1957. The GT exercise was not confined to coupes, as between '57 and '58, a number of elegant yet purposeful two-seater sports spiders were built. Bodied by Boano and Pinin Farina, these cabriolets used the platform and running gear of the 250 GTs, and some versions had fared-in headlights. The gorgeous 250 GT Spider California – a more rakish car, designed by Pinin Farina but bodied by Scaglietti (sometimes in aluminium) – was in production from '58 to '62. These cars were often well-placed in competition, witness Ginther/Hively's 9th place and GT class winner in the Sebring 12 Hours of 1959 and Grossman/Tavano's 5th overall at Le Mans the same year. In 1958, Pinin Farina moved from his Corso Trapani workshops in Turin to a new factory at Grugliasco on the outskirts of the city, changing his name to Pininfarina at the same time. He then embarked on the second series 250 GT, a rakish, almost angular coupe.

The Series 2 version of the 250 GT cabriolet made from 1959 to 1962 was a less exciting looking car. Its two-plus-two relative, the 250 GT 2+2, debuted as course car at the 1960 Le Mans race, giving Ferrari his first proper four-seater. By moving the engine forward, Pininfarina found enough space for modest rear seats. During the model's three year production run, some 950 cars were built, establishing Ferrari as a builder of proper grown-up GT cars. It was also the end of production for the classic 250 GT, although there was a limited run – 80 units – of the 250 GT Berlinetta Lusso, a competition derivative built by Scaglietti.

In its place came the beautifully streamlined 250 GT Pininfarina Berlinetta or GT/L. Again, Scaglietti did the bodies, and this was the first Ferrari to feature the cut-off back end, an aerodynamic aid 'invented' by Dr Wunnibald Kamm in the early '50s and subsequently known as the Kamm-tail. When production of this model finished in 1964, some 2500 250 GTs and derivatives had been built.

This car was superseded by the 330 GT 2+2, which was really a 250 GT with the lightly modified 400 Superamerica engine installed. The 'Commendatore' himself had the first one, and by the time it was phased out in 1967, a thousand units had been built. There were a few variants, including a cabriolet for Chinetti by Michelotti, and a bizarre Vignale estate car done in 1968, but in general, the only significant stylistic change was the dropping of one set of the paired headlights, fashionable when the model first came out. By '65, alloy wheels were beginning to replace the ubiquitous Borrani wires, and at the same time, a five-speed all synchromesh gearbox was fitted instead of the overdrive.

An indication of the levels of sophistication creature comforts had reached was the option of power steering and air conditioning..What many regard as the ultimate classic Ferrari was launched at the Geneva show in 1964. The 500 Superfast used the more conservative of the Superamerica Coupe Aerodinamico body styles, with slight revisions such as a more truncated tail and no farings on the headlights. The new

If you're still not satisfied with the F40's get-up-and-go, a 700bhp 'competition pack' is available to really sort out the conservatives from the over-achievers. This includes bigger turbos, larger intercoolers, higher-lift cams, plus a gearbox with a dog-clutch to replace the regular all-synchromesh five-speed version

Left
The F40 bodywork is modified to accommodate even more rubber

Above
The trailing edge has sprouted another wing to add downforce at extreme velocities

engine was a marriage of Lampredi and Columbo V12, with a capacity of just under 5.0-litres. The opulent finish of the interior was rather at odds with the potential performance, and its exclusivity can be gauged by the fact that only 25 Series 1 and 12 Series 2 500 Superfasts were built. Customers included the Shah of Iran, the Aga Khan and Peter Sellers. An interim model, the 365 California, was designed and built by Pininfarina in 1966-67. Powered by a single-cam 4.4-litre V12, it was an elegant cabriolet with fared-in headlights, the familiar banana-esque quarter bumpers, and angular rear treatment used by Pininfarina in his design for Fiat's far less exalted 124 Spider. As the void widened between sports racing cars and road going sports cars, Ferrari strove to bridge the gap. In 1964, the 275 GTB and 275GTS came out; the '66 GTB of Pianta/Lippi has the distinction of being the only Ferrari ever to have been entered for the Monte Carlo Rally. The 275 GTB/4 was the first Ferrari GT car

Above left
Evoluzione: rearward vision is provided by streamlined mirrors mounted on the perspex side windows

Left
Ventilation is gained by sliding open the little perspex trapdoor fitted in the side windows – they don't wind down any more

Above
The Evoluzione is a mean looking weapon, its purpose clearly stated – to go as fast as possible. It represents the ultimate challenge to the sporting driver, especially on a race circuit. It can be guided with the most delicate input from the driver. The self-centring is reliable, but occasionally a firm hand is required, say on a road peppered with craters, or when the tyres tramline on white lines

to have a four-cam engine, necessitating a slight longitudinal bonnet bulge. It was succeeded by the 375 GTB/4, better known as the Daytona, which ran from 1968 to 1973. The long-bonneted Pininfarina-designed, Scaglietti-built body was mounted on a typical Ferrari chassis of oval-section tubes. The 4.4-litre V12 used six Weber carbs and was mated to the rear-mounted five-speed transaxle by a rigid drive-shaft tube. An open Spider version was launched in 1969. This in effect replaced the 275GTS of 1964 and its decendents the 330 GTS and 365 GTS, which was the most prolific Ferrari convertible range, with 330 units built. Contemporary grand tourers were the 4.0-litre, short-wheelbase 330GTC and 365 GTC, from 1966 to 1970, followed by the elegant 4.4-litre 365 GT 2+2, in production from 1967 to 1971. Next in Ferrari chronology came the 365 GTC/4, a two-plus two combining the frontal styling cues of the Daytona with a gentler rear end. It was a short-lived model, preceding the 365 GT4 2+2 of 1972, the shape of which was virtually identical to the Ferrari 400 and 412 2+2, which lasted as Ferrari's 'limousine' model until 1992.

Handling behaviour is wonderfully compliant; turn-in is spot on, and you can alter direction with the throttle, by feeding in more fuel to get the nose out, or backing off, to make the nose come into an apex

The modern world

The rear-engine revolution of circa 1960 which inspired sports racers such as the P4, also brought us the little 1987cc V6 Dino 206, 246 GT and 246 GTS, produced from 1967 to 1974. The first proper mid-engined road going Ferraris, they have one of the most delectably curvaceous body styles ever created. Predictably, the honours go to Pininfarina and Scaglietti. Nuccio Bertone made his name styling Alfa Romeos like the Giulietta and Montreal, but he produced a workable solution to the mid-engined two-plus-two concept in 1973 with the 3.0-litre V8-engined Ferrari 308 GT4. It was the first production Ferrari to be styled by someone other than Pininfarina since 1953. In production until 1980, Ferrari made some 2826 of the 308 GT4s. Thus it is a rarer proposition than the 308 GTB/308 GTS and 328 GTB which came along next. What really made the 308 GT4 so innovative was its transverse, mid-mounted 90-degree V8 engine with the bonus of two usable rear seats. The four overhead camshafts were driven by a couple of toothed belts, a departure from the traditional chain-driven cams which remained a feature of the V12s.

The 308GTB was announced at the Paris Show in 1975, and is arguably the first of the 'modern' Ferraris – in that the uninitiated would

Above
The shift pattern is neat and precise – some would call it knotchy as it clicks noisily through the gate – and the gear lever requires a firm hand; in reality, pressure comes from the shoulder and the action is deliberate and tight

Above right
In the interests of lightness, the windows in the Evoluzione car are fixed with no winding mechanism, and due to the broader wings, rear mirrors have shifted position to the window level

Right
The appearance of the F40 is changed with a slatted grille and front air dam. The side-light pods are set in the edges of the wing, with driving lights now prominent at the front

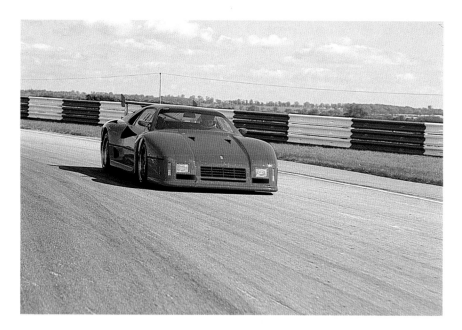

probably be hard pressed to date it so far in advance of the 348 which came 15 years later. But its debut coincided with Niki Lauda's victory in the Formula One World Championship in the 312T. Ferrari's brief flirtation with Bertone was a one-model fling, and he returned to Pininfarina for the 308 GTB; bodies for all the six- and eight-cylinder cars were made by Scaglietti. The main features were its retractable headlights, sail-panel buttresses tailing off to the rear of the car, and concave cone-shaped scallops providing air vents along the flanks either side. The 308 GTS was first shown at the 1977 Frankfurt Show, and was effectively the same body but with a removable targa roof panel, stored behind the seats. Lubrication, which on European cars had been dry sump, returned to the conventional wet sump system.

Ferrari's first flat-12 motor was running in the final season of the 1500cc Formula One in 1965, and was upped to 2.0-litres in 1969 to power the successful 121/E spider European hill-climb car. As a 3.0-litre unit it was fitted to the 312B Formula One car, and powered the 1972

Above
The brakes are mighty powerful, as you'd expect, but they need an equally hefty shove on the pedal to produce the desired response

Right
The Evoluzone at rest in the pit lane at Norfolk's fast Snetterton circuit – ready for the off, and a sight to make even the most experienced driving heart accelerate

World Championship of Makes winning 312P. While the V12 was Columbo-based, the Flat-12 was based on the design of Mauro Forghieri, Ferrari's brilliant team manager and long-term race strategist. Cast in light alloy Silumin, the flat-12 block was in itself a delightful piece of sculpture. It was fitted with shrunk-in cast-iron cylinder liners, light alloy pistons – as used in the V12s – and a crankshaft machined from a solid billet of chromed molybdenum steel, running in seven main bearings. The first production 'boxer' flat-12 was the 365 GT4 BB, which had its 4.4-litre motor mounted amidships. Its thirst was quenched by four triple-choke Weber carbs. The flat-12 cylinder configuration should have made a lower body possible, but with the transmission located underneath the engine, that particular advantage was lost. The chassis was essentially similar in principal to that of the Dinos, which consisted of a tubular framework of square-section steel tube, faced on each side by sheet steel; similar tubular subframes front and rear cradled the engine and steering assembly and pedal box, as well as carrying wishbone suspension pick-up points and the mounting points for roof windscreen.

Above
Those louvres are reminiscent of the glorious 275 GTB of 1964

Left
The vent in the trailing edge of the front panel is to allow heat from the front brakes to escape

Although it was shown at the Turin Show in 1971, the 365 GT4 BB
didn't go into production for another two years. Bodywork was in steel,
with alloy front panel, doors and engine cover, and it was a more radical
proposition than its contemporary, the Daytona. The air scoops which
were so prominent a feature on mid-engined Ferraris were not used on
the 365 GT4 BB because Pininfarina had found in wind tunnel tests that
the aerodynamics of the rear body section allowed sufficient quantities of
cooling air to be ducted into the engine from the top. The BB concept
was taken a stage further in 1976 with the 512 BB, which bore a strong
visual similarity to its 308 GTB sibling. In 1979 it received fuel injection,
and straight-cut gears for competition purposes. Ferrari's next shot at a
four-seater was the Mondial 8, launched in 1980, which performed and
felt like a regular 308 GT4 grand tourer, but with its stretched
appearance – an extra four inches – looked slightly ungainly for a mid-

engined car. That it was in production throughout the '80s says much for its conceptual correctness.

The cracking 288 GTO of 1984 was an homologation special – the O stood for Omologato – produced in just enough numbers to qualify as a production racer. It wore similar bodywork to the 308 GTB, and the 2.8-litre V8 was equipped with twin turbochargers, giving a top speed of 190mph. Around the same time the 512 BB became known as the Testarossa.

And then comes the moment we've been building up to: in 1988, Ferrari launched the F40 to an awe-struck motoring audience. Enthusiasts were delighted by the stunning lines, for this was something quite radical; a virtual competition car let loose on the public highway. The notion of such a car was born in 1986 – to celebrate Ferrari's 40th Anniversary as a manufacturer demanded something pretty special, as we shall see a little later on. Writing in Car magazine in November 1989, journalists Giancarlo Perini and Jose Rosinski described the F40 as 'the

Above
Slatted rear window is different from the standard car – it's louvres are larger with a view to more ventilation over the engine

Right
Not quite a clear run up the Snetterton pit lane yet – but once the twin turbo V8 wails into life, there'll be no problem

fastest, the most exhilarating, the most demanding, the daftest, the most valuable, the least comfortable, the best handling, the most stable at speed, the least practical; the nearest thing to a no-compromise supercar.' The other cars stacked up against the F40 in their group test were the Lamborghini Countach run-out 25th Anniversary model, the underdeveloped Cizeta Moroder, and the high-tech, four-wheel-drive Porsche 959. The two bulky Italian wedges occupied the middle ground, being exceedingly fast but offering compromises to the driver's comfort and thus negating out and out handling prowess; the 959 was thought to be the safest and surest, making it the least exciting, while the F40 was 'frenzied and raw.'

New in 1990, the Ferrari 348tb is powered by the quad-cam 3.4-litre 32-valve V8, which is good for 300bhp. Visually less aggressive and exciting than the F40, the 348ti is altogether more opulent in its fittings and creature comforts. In January 1992, the replacement for the flagship Testarossa was the 512TR, still powered by the fabulous 4.9-litre flat-12 and sporting a virtually identical body to the glorious red-head. Like all the Testa Rossas, the cam covers are finished in red, and to reinforce the point, so are the tops of the injection manifolding. Wider than a Transit van, the low, flat 512's frontal aspect was changed to give it a family resemblance to the 348, but the extravagant straked air intakes which are the Testarossa's key styling hallmarks remained. It was endowed with more grunt – from 390bhp to 421bhp – to bring it on more level terms with the Lamborghini Diablo – there has always been a tacit rivalry between the two firms, even though the Sant'Agata firm has no competition heritage. The latest Ferrari to hit the streets is the 456GT, which achieves what no other representative of the marque has managed before, which is to be both eminently chuckable, fabulously powerful, and yet remain a true grand tourer. It is a four-seater, so the introduction of self-levelling suspension is a bonus if the car is fully laden. The 5.4-litre, 48-valve quad-cam V12 engine is front-mounted in the tradition of the Daytona, and delivers 442bhp. This gives it a top speed of 194mph and a 0-60mph time of 5.2secs, placing it in the same league as its 512 and 348 siblings. As a four-seater, it knocks the Mondial and old 412 for six. But when all's said and done, it's a touring car, and for the ultimate driving experience, there's nothing to beat the F40. Except maybe its offspring, the Evoluzione.

There's no ABS – and traditionally, competition drivers frown on such assistance, preferring the direct feel of a heavy pedal. You know where you are with that, and it's also good for heel-and-toe double-declutching

Above
The Evoluzione comes to bits more readily than the normal F40, and the front panel is removed for access to radiator, battery and brake cooling ducts

Above right
It's a two-man job fitting the front panel back on – light as it is. And Snetterton can be a very windy circuit

Right
No ripples in this composite panel. The Ferrari badge is far more discreet than the car it identifies

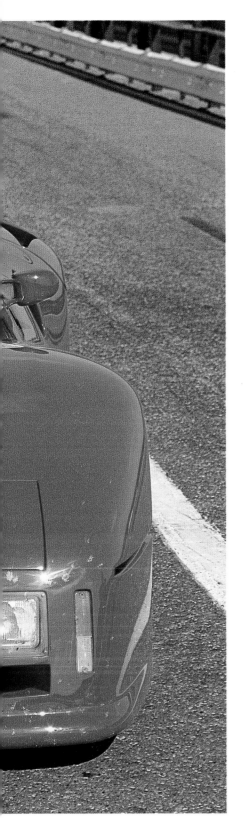

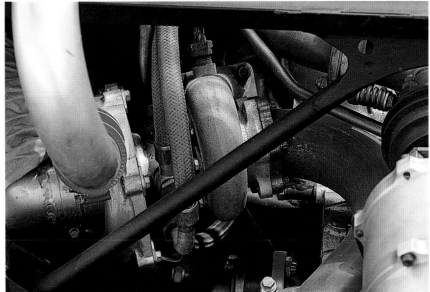

Top
The cockpit of a competition car gets exceedingly hot, so some fresh air is vital. This is all the Evoluzione driver is allowed – during a race, normal windows may not be opened, so this is a compromise

Left
Broad shouldered or what? The Evoluzione has a more chunky appearance than the lithe F40

Above
Complex plumbing for the two IHI turbochargers which service each bank of cylinders

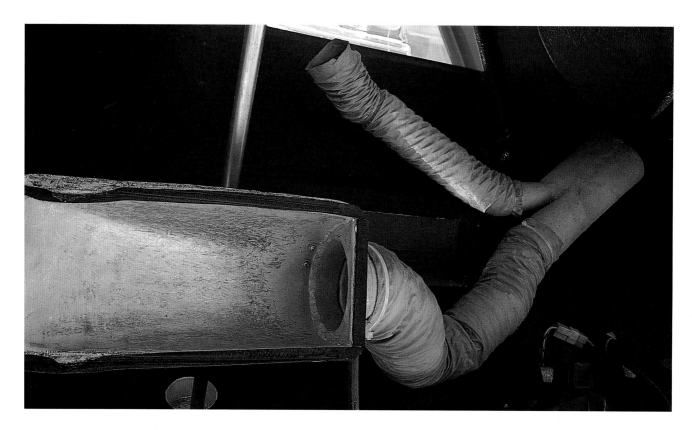

Above

Cooling channels appear crudely made, but this is often the case with competition cars, where new ideas are tried out – and sometimes rejected – before being absorbed into regular production models

Above right

Gone are the niceties of the F40's road-going silencer; the Evoluzione has a more rudimentary competition exhaust system

Right

Dry-sump catch tank and cross-bracing of rearmost section of the spaceframe, supporting the rear valance, can be seen with the engine cover removed

Left
Even the manifolding is a work of art. Coil springs and dampers supplement wishbone suspension all round

Above
Somewhere under those massive intercoolers lurks the Evoluzione's V8 engine

Above
Cooling louvres don't come much bigger than these

Right
Coil spring and Koni damper unit contribute towards the firm, responsive ride

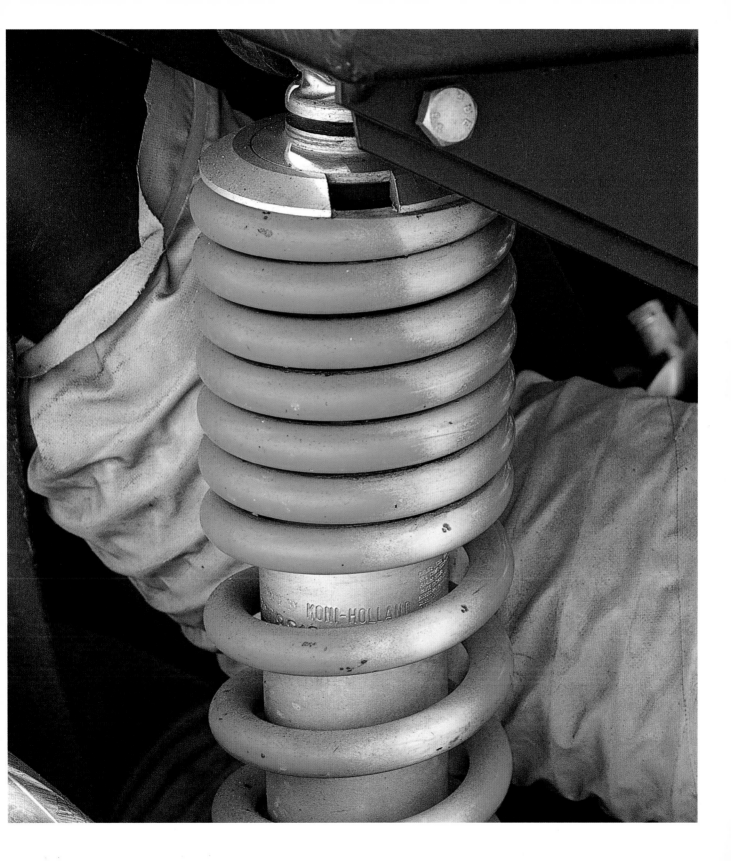

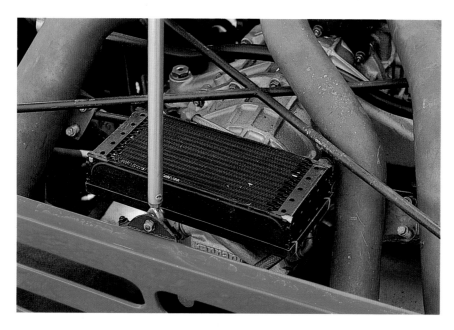

Above
On top of the transmission casing sits an oil cooler, straddled by the exhaust pipes and cross-bracing

Right
Anatomy of the Evoluzione's front end revealed: the clutch and brake fluid reservoirs, battery, water radiator and related pipework, plus cooling ducts for the brakes; and not a spacesaver to be seen

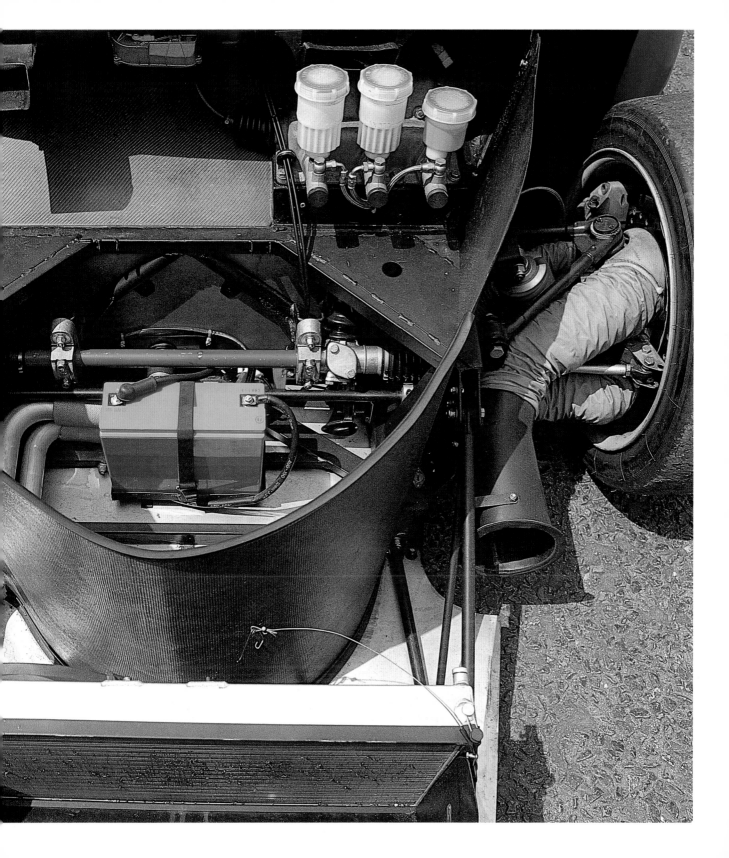

Above
Brake and clutch pedals are drilled for lightness, while accelerator pedal is big enough to dance on – which is what happens during heel-and-toe gear changes

Left
The central tunnel is missing, and the shift and linkage stands rather awkwardly on its own

Right
Evoluzione's auxiliary dials are faced in red, and air-con vents are absent. So far the F40 driver would still feel at home

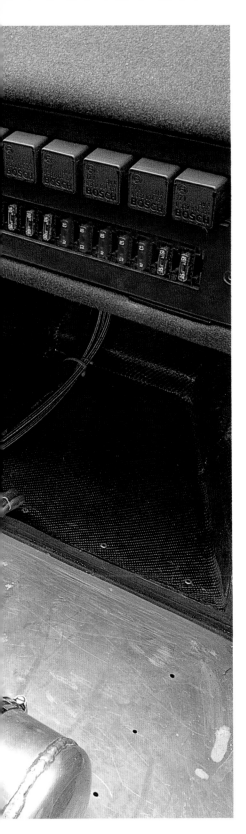

Above

If you thought the F40 was spartan, the Evoluzione makes no concessions whatsoever to creature comforts: the door trim has been stripped out, and there's just a wire to open it

Left

Ahead of the passenger seat on the bare aluminium floorpan is a fire extinguisher system, all plumbed in and ready for action in the event of a disaster

Above

The Momo wheel looks the same. But there's one gauge missing from the instrument binnacle. No speedometer, as all the driver needs to know in a race situation is how hard he's revving the engine

Right

The essence of a competition car is that not one iota of space is wasted – and even the area between the wishbones is taken up by cooling ducts

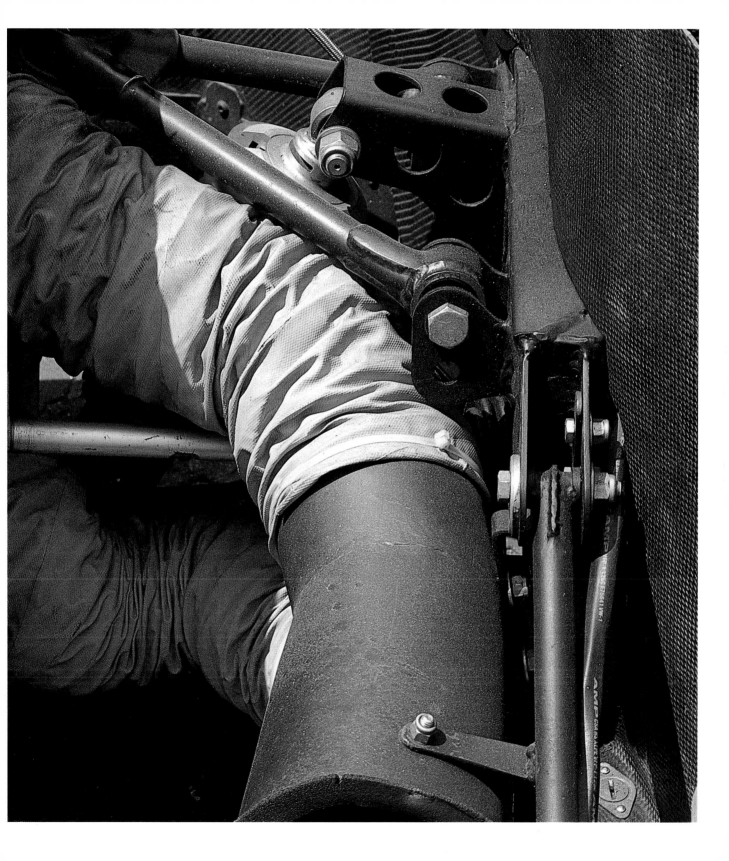

Above
*Front wishbones have the spring and damper unit passing at an angle between them;
that of the rear is taken off the side of the top wishbone*

Right
*Where you'd normally expect to see a modest space saver, there is only a collection of
vital ancillaries*

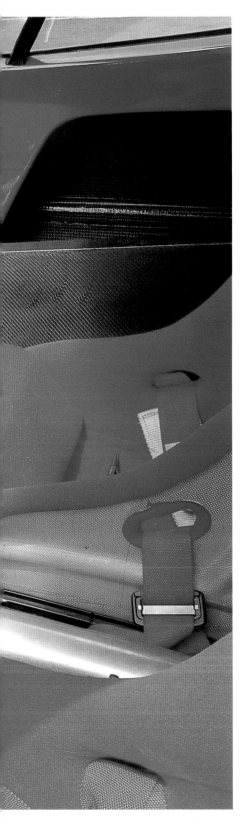

Above
There are an awful lot of vents, air intakes and louvres in the Evoluzione bodywork. Functional they may be, but they only serve to enhance its race track image

Left
Austerity rules in the cockpit of the Evoluzione – but it looks so inviting nevertheless

Right
Beneath the full-race harness and tucked away behind the seats can be found the Magneti Marelli electronic engine management system

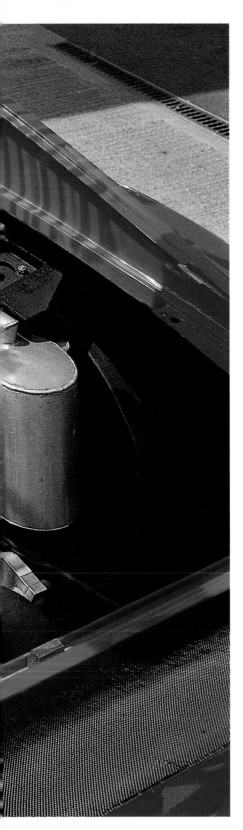

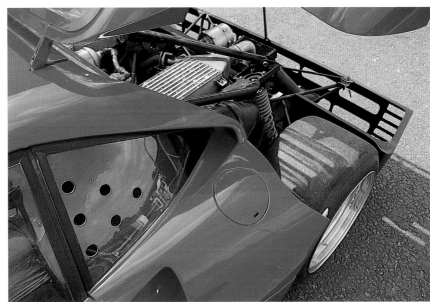

Above
The rear three-quarter window is drilled both for lightness and for ventilation

Left
Evoluzione engine cover with just the window section removed

Above
Fuel fillers remain in their rightful place

Right
Huge one-piece front section of Evoluzione bodywork lifts off

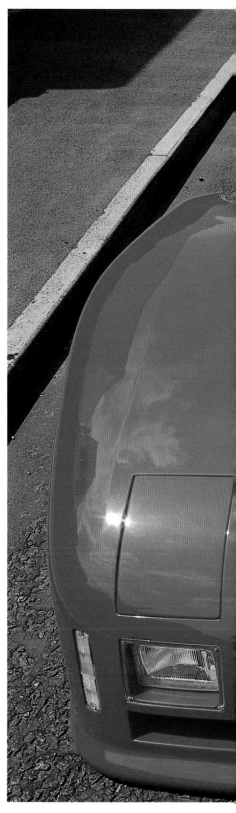

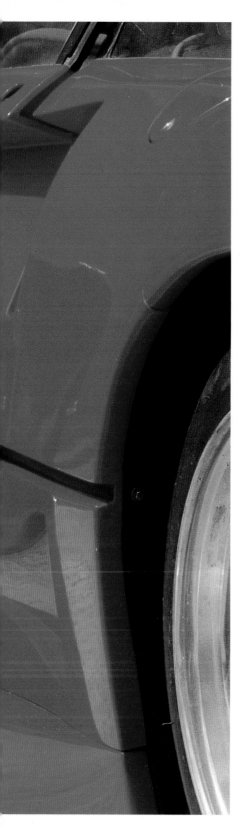

Above

More like a NASA space craft than a Ferrari, the Evoluzione's rear view is a mass of cooling apertures

Left

Broader wheel rims , fatter wings and side skirts alter the F40's stance. Running on slick tires, the Evoluzione could only be classified as a sports-racing car in the specific Ferrari mould

Left

Precursor to the F40 and Evoluzione: the 288 GTO of 1984 can be classified as an homologation special – the O stood for Omologato, and it was produced in just enough numbers to qualify it as a Group B production racer

Above

The GTO was clad in similar bodywork to its stablemate, the older 308 GTB, and the 2.8-litre V8 was equipped with twin turbochargers, giving a top speed of 189mph

Above
Launched at the Geneva Show in 1984, the GTO is powered by a 2855cc V8 engine, which produced 400bhp

Right
The GTO's swooping curves hark back to the P4 racing prototype of '67

Above

The twin turbo system is mounted towards the rear of the engine compartment, over the transmission; the single wastegate located between them has its own exhaust outlet. The pair of air-to-air intercoolers which sit above each cylinder bank cool the charge as it passes to the twin inlet manifold. Engine management is monitored by two Weber-Marelli electronic ignition and injection systems, serving one cylinder bank each

Right

The 2.8-litre four-overhead cam V8 is mounted longitudinally behind the cabin and ahead of the rear wheels in keeping with true sports-racing practice. The twin intercoolers for the IHI turbochargers are prominent, and the overall layout resembles that employed on the turbocharged Ferrari 126C Formula One cars

Above
Its chin spoiler thrust forward, the GTO's nose also contains two pairs of driving lamps

Right
The GTO is nothing if not a dramatic performer on the road: it dispatches the standing start quarter mile in 12.7 seconds, and reaches a terminal speed in excess of 190mph. And for the record, its 0-60mph time is 4.9 seconds

Above
Cooling vents interestingly positioned aft of the headlight recess – an excellent piece of design

Right
There's not much difference between the rakish angle of the screen and the front 'bonnet' of the car

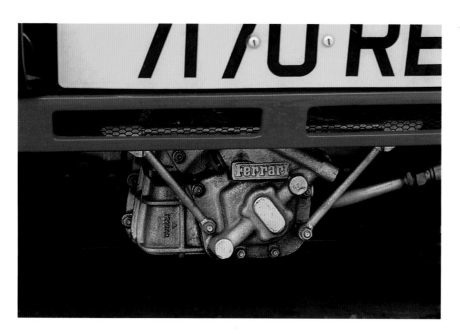

Above
Rear of the GTO's transmission is almost level with the rear valance

Right
Spacesaver exposed. But there's not a lot of room for luggage when putting a GTO to its proper use – that's going touring in style

Above
Few other initials evoke such pangs of awe and respect as those of the GTO

Right
Front-hinged boot cover is more manageable than the F40 – but you don't have such direct access to the underpinnings

Above
If it's louvres you want, the GTO engine cover's got plenty – in fact it almost matches the Morgan Plus 8

Left
Three auxiliary dials plus a trio of air vents occupy the centre of the GTO's black trimmed dashboard

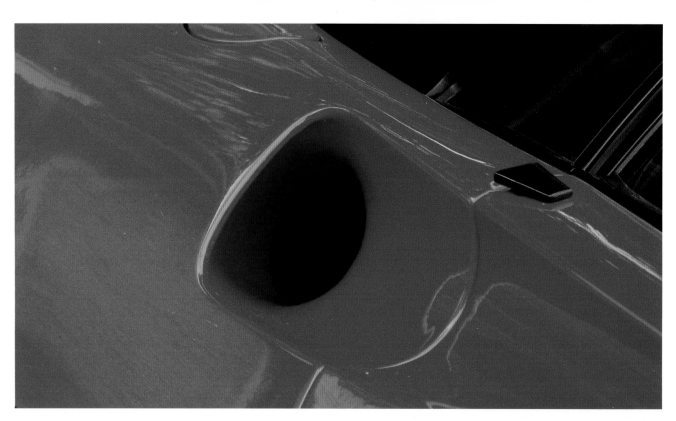

Above left
Looking like some Modernist piece of sculpture, the elegant scallop in the GTO's flanks directs cooling air into the engine bay

Left
Red and amber, the rear light cluster is borrowed from the Fiat corporate parts bin

Above
True to form, the mid-engined GTO has the concave flute in its side, leading to the air intake

Above
Perhaps rather surprisingly, the louvred engine cover is actually hinged at the rear of the engine bay

Right
Centre console is busier than F40's, containing the traditional gear shift and chromed gate, switchgear and ignition cut-out – a competition requirement

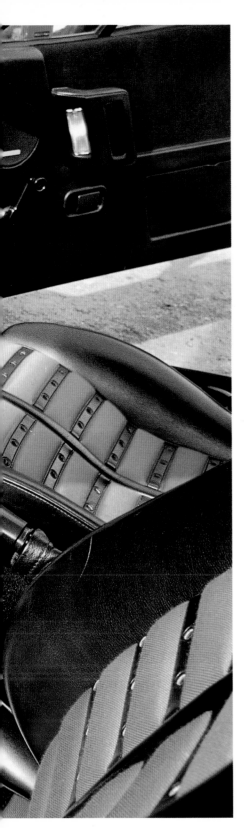

Above

You could be forgiven for thinking you were looking at a 275 GTB of 1965 – but it's an '84 GTO

Left

Momo wheel has prancing horse boss, and red striped seat upholstery relieves what would otherwise be a dark cabin. The Ferrari emblem extends to the carpets – a marque of distinction

Above
Progression of rear-end treatment: the GTO has but a shallow spoiler compared with the winged F40, and the towering aerofoil on the Evoluzione

Left
Three Ferraris spanning a decade: the 288 GTO of 1984, the F40 of 1988, and its development, the Evoluzione of 1993. They are closely related under the skin

Above and overleaf

Having fun on the back straight at Snetterton, the F40 and Evoluzione go for maximum speed – but it won't last long before they have to anchor up! Even a race track has its limitations for such powerful cars

Right

As for the rear (see previous page), frontal treatment is different, reflecting the transition from the GTO's fundamentally 1970s design to the mid-'80s F40, and its competition derivation in the Evoluzione

F40 SPECIFICATIONS

In production: 1988 to 1992

Chassis: Square-section tubular steel framework with composites bonded to it using structural adhesive.
Body: Composite materials; principally Kevlar.
Engine: Ferrari 2936cc twin-turbocharged, four-cam V8. Water-cooled.
Transmission: Ferrari, five forward gears, plus reverse.
Turbos: Twin IHI turbos, each delivering 16psi boost through a separate Behr intercooler.
Original price in UK: £160,000.
Engine management system: Weber Marelli electronic ignition and injection
Maximum Power: 478bhp at 7000rpm.
Height: 3ft 8in

Length: 14ft 6in
Width: 6ft 6in
Unladen weight: 2425lb
Drag coefficient: 0.34Cd.
Maximum speed: 201mph
Acceleration; 0-60mph: 4.5 seconds.
Power-to-weight ratio: 450bhp per ton.
Suspension: Double wishbones front and rear, with coil springs and Koni dampers
Brakes: Four-pot caliper Brembo disc brakes all round.
Steering: Ferrari, unassisted rack-and-pinion.
Tyres: 335/35 ZR x 17 (13 inch wheel rim width) rear; 245/40 ZR 17 (8 inch wheel rim width) front; Pirelli P-Zero, Goodyear Eagle GS-A, Michelin MXX, or Bridgestone RE-71s.